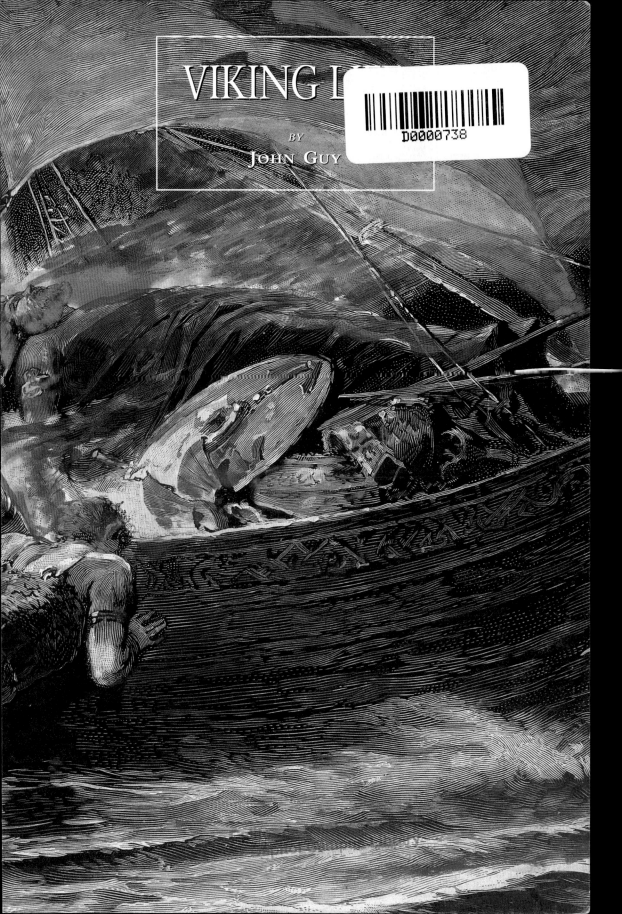

VIKING L...

BY

JOHN GUY

Who Were the Vikings?

The very word "Viking" conjures up images of fierce, uncivilized warriors and pirates who attacked and wrought havoc on the Christian countries of Europe from the 8th to the 11th century, but they are a much misunderstood people, and it is not easy to unravel the truth from legend. To begin with they were not peoples from one land but from three: Denmark, Norway, and Sweden, coming from an area of northern Europe known as Scandinavia. However, there was no unity, and wars among these three Viking nations were common. The word "Viking" is a general term (possibly derived from the word "vig" which means "fighting," or "vik" which means "creek") to describe all Scandinavians of this time. Another more accurate term is Norsemen (meaning men from the North). Although they did lead piratical raids against the Christian countries of Europe, the Vikings were not uncivilized barbarians. They were excellent navigators, great traders, and were skilled in the arts of metalwork and carpentry.

EXPERT NAVIGATORS

The Vikings were expert seamen. They used large, low-sided boats called longships. They were very sleek, fast vessels, propelled by a combination of a central sail and oars. Each oarsman hung his shield over the side as protection from attack.

RUNIC WRITING

The Vikings developed a unique form of writing called runes. Some of the very angular letters were based on the Greek alphabet, while others were entirely invented. Runes were inscribed onto special stones, along with pictograms, and were used in religious rituals. Most Vikings would not have been able to read and write, but they had a rich tradition in storytelling, especially epic poetry and heroic sagas.

MAP OF THE VIKING WORLD

The Vikings did not usually conquer countries with the intent of ruling them but preferred simply to colonize lands of their choosing. Their domains were centered on Scandinavia, eastern Russia, Britain, northern France, Iceland, and southern Italy. They also established settlements in Greenland, Newfoundland, and other parts of North America for a short period in the 11th century.

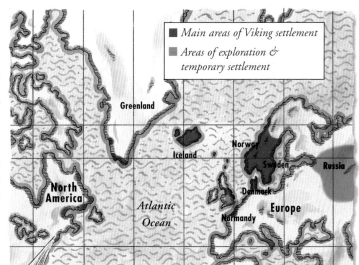

■ *Main areas of Viking settlement*
■ *Areas of exploration & temporary settlement*

Greenland

Norway

Iceland

Sweden

Russia

North America

Denmark

Atlantic Ocean

Normandy

Europe

SIGN OF PRESTIGE

This solid silver armband shows how skilled Vikings were as metalworkers. Both men and women loved to wear decorative jewelry, such as brooches, armbands, rings, and necklaces. Wearing fine jewelry was an outward sign of a person's wealth.

WARRIOR RACE

Viking warriors were among the fiercest (and most feared) ever known. Most of their attacks took the form of raids using hit-and-run tactics. Coastal towns were most vulnerable, as were remote and isolated monasteries, such as Lindisfarne in Northumberland, rich in gold and treasures, which the Vikings freely plundered. Gradually, they established semi-permanent bases from which to launch attacks further inland.

SUPERSTITION

The Vikings were a very superstitious people and worshipped many gods. These gods were given human personalities, and Norse mythology is rich in tales of their heroic deeds. This small bronze statuette dates from about A.D. 1000 and shows Thor, god of thunder.

Life for the Rich

Viking society was, in general, quite free and liberated. Although wealth and status could be inherited (usually from father to eldest son), it was possible for warriors of quite lowly status to rise up the social scale simply by acquiring money and treasure on raiding expeditions. Such behavior was perfectly acceptable to the Vikings. Also, unlike the rich in other societies, wealthy Vikings continued to take part in expeditions, equipping themselves with fine armor and weapons. Wealthy Vikings often employed slaves (usually captured on raids) to do the menial work around the house and on the land. The typical home of a rich Viking was a large, timbered hall where the entire household lived, ate, and slept together. Many, who had acquired their wealth by stealing from foreign lands, buried their treasure in secret hiding places rather than risk having it stolen from them. These hoards are still being unearthed today and can tell us much about Viking society.

STATUS SYMBOL

This beautiful enamel brooch, decorated with precious stones and dating back to the 7th century, would probably have been used to fasten a chieftain's cloak at the shoulder. Fine jewelry showed a Viking's wealth as well as status.

FINE WEAPONS

A Viking's position in society could be told as much by the quality of his weapons as by the cut of his clothes. The pride of every Viking warrior was his sword. They were usually made of iron but with decorative inlays of silver, brass, or even gold on the hilts (handles). The more wealthy the warrior, the more valuable was his sword.

BURIALS

Vikings believed in an afterlife and were often buried with familiar objects and valuables in preparation for their journey after death. Wealthy Vikings were often buried with their ships, and it is from their rediscovery by modern archaeologists that we have learned so much about everyday Viking life. Sometimes the ships were buried within mounds, while others were set on fire. Some may even have been cast adrift and then set on fire.

VIKING HALLS

Viking halls resemble huge, upturned boats, which may, indeed, have been their original source of inspiration. The roofs inside are a forest of timbers that look similar to the trusses of a boat, while outside the roofline follows the same gentle curve of a ship's keel. This fine example of a nobleman's house is a reconstruction built in Trelleborg, Denmark, in 1948.

HIDDEN TREASURE

Wealthy Vikings often acquired many valuable objects, but they did not put these on open display, as is the modern custom. Instead, they locked their valuables away inside strong wooden chests, such as this one made from oak with iron fittings. It was the woman's responsibility to look after the chest, usually wearing the key on a chain around her neck. Anyone caught stealing from a locked chest was severely punished.

ACQUIRED WEALTH

Many of the most valuable items in a wealthy Viking's house were stolen during raids to other lands. This silver and gilt chalice may have come originally from a Christian monastery. However, Vikings were skilled metalworkers in their own right, though only the rich could afford to buy such items.

MEASURE OF WEALTH

Viking farmers relied on grazing animals for much of their food, including sheep, cattle, pigs, and even reindeer. Because land could not be freely bought and sold, the measure of a man's wealth was often made in the number of animals he kept. Common breeds of cattle, such as longhorns or Wild Park (shown here), were especially adapted to the harsh, northerly climate.

HOME FROM HOME

The Vikings used whatever materials were freely at hand to build their houses. They felt most at home with wood, but this was not always available. In the Scottish islands, such as the Shetlands and Orkneys, where there is virtually no tree cover, houses were constructed of the loose boulders that lay everywhere across the landscape. Walls were usually very thick to keep out the north winds, often unmortared and with turf roofs. Houses there, and in Greenland and Iceland, were often circular, with few window openings. In other areas, most houses of the poor were made of upright wooden posts (staves) with thatched roofs.

HOME COMFORTS

This reconstruction (left) shows the interior of a typical Viking house. There was usually only one main room, where the entire family lived, ate, and slept. In the center was an open fire where they cooked their food, the smoke escaping through an open louver in the roof. Furniture would have been kept to a minimum, probably consisting of a table, stools, and beds only. Their cooking utensils were basic, as this earthenware bowl shows.

Life for the Poor

Viking society was divided into three main classes: slaves, freemen, and nobles, known respectively as thralls, karls, and jarls. Many of the slaves were captured in raids to foreign lands, while others became slaves through bad debt or crime. Much of the menial work was done by slaves, and they had few rights. At the other end of the scale were nobles, who were few in number, but controlled large areas as overlords, responsible to the king. In between were freemen, which included farmers, traders, craftsmen, and warriors. The vast majority of people were freemen. They mostly farmed their own land, but strict inheritance laws meant land was always scarce. Land was held in tenure and could not normally be sold or given away. It passed from father to eldest son, which meant any other sons had to seek their own land. It was this need for more land, especially among the poor, that first drove the Vikings overseas to seize property abroad.

MILITARY SERVICE

There was no organized army, but everyone was expected to fight for their king or local chieftain when necessary. Most warriors were poor farmers who joined raiding expeditions to gain land, or a share in any treasure seized, to improve their situation.

A NATION OF FARMERS

Most Vikings were farmers, not warriors, and tending the farm was a family affair. Much of the land was either forested or mountainous, making it difficult to farm, and the northerly latitude of the Viking homelands meant that the growing season was short.

Food and Drink

Most Vikings ate reasonably well. Although they mostly lived a subsistence form of existence on individual family-run farms, food was seldom in short supply. When crops failed or a family fell on hard times, there was an abundance of wildlife to be hunted, including birds, rabbits, and deer. Vikings were opportunist hunters, so when crops failed, most could gather what they needed to survive from the wild. Although, by no means did they live in a classless society, there were fewer divisions between rich and poor; both rich and poor ate basically the same foods, the rich simply ate better, with more variety. Meat featured strongly in the Viking diet, as did fish. Vegetables, such as cabbages, beans, garlic, and peas, were mostly used to make stews. Knives were usually the only implement used at the table. Beer made from barley was the most common drink, though the rich imported wine from the peoples of Germany, France, and Italy.

A DELICACY

Most Vikings lived close to the coast, where there were large colonies of sea birds, such as black-headed gulls, shown here. They roasted the birds and also gathered their eggs, which were considered a great delicacy. Ducks and geese were also eaten.

ABUNDANT SEAS

Not surprisingly for a seafaring people, fish formed an essential part of the Viking diet, including herring, haddock, trout, and cod (shown here). Fish was available throughout the year and were either grilled or smoked. Fish oil was also used as a supplement.

FIT FOR A KING

This picture shows a typical banquet scene in a noble household in the 11th century. Several courses were served in finely decorated metal dishes. Meals were eaten in the communal great hall, with the chieftain and his family sitting at the head table.

SHEPHERDS

The Vikings farmed several breeds of hardy
sheep able to cope with harsh terrain and the
cold, northern climate. The Hebridean Black
and Manx Loghton (now rare breeds) both shed
their coats naturally. In addition to eating their meat,
sheep horns were hollowed out and used as drinking vessels.

HARDY BREEDS

Vikings farmed several
breeds of animal, including
sheep, pigs, geese, deer, horses, poultry,
and cows. They were kept for both
food and materials (such as their hides
and bones). The cow shown here is a
longhorn, now a rare breed. Farm
animals then were considerably
smaller than many modern breeds.
They were also much more hardy
and able to survive harsh
conditions. Cattle were also
used for pulling the plough
in arable fields. At the onset
of winter, when fodder was
particularly scarce, many
animals were slaughtered
in an annual cull. Meat
was preserved by salting
down. The salt was
acquired by laboriously
boiling sea water in flat
pans. As the water
evaporated a thin salty
deposit was left in the pan.

SKIN AND BONE

Deer meat (venison) was an important part of the
Viking diet. Elk, red deer, and reindeer all lived
wild in herds throughout the Viking world,
although sometimes they were farmed like sheep. The skins
were used to make clothing and blankets; the bones and
antlers for making tools, combs, and
decorative ornaments.

Music, dancing, and singing featured strongly in Viking entertainment. Even in ordinary households folk songs were sung by the whole family. Richer people sometimes employed the services of professional musicians and singers to perform at special banquets. Popular instruments of the time were lyres, harps, and flutes.

The unusual instrument shown here is a "lur," a wind instrument from Denmark. It is an S-shaped trumpet, made of bronze. They are still used today in some parts of Scandinavia to call cattle.

Vikings liked to work hard, fight hard, and play hard. When the day's work was done (be it toiling in the fields or soldiering) the evenings were often reserved for feasting. A great sense of community spirit existed in the Viking world, and often the whole village would congregate at the chieftain's hall for an evening of eating, drinking, and entertainment. After the meal, epic poems about legendary heroes or stories of the gods were recited aloud (mostly from memory, although the nobles employed professional poets called "skalds"), and the whole community joined in rousing songs and dancing. At special banquets jesters and musicians would also entertain the people. As the evening wore on the behavior probably became more riotous. Other popular pastimes were combative sports, such as wrestling and fencing.

EQUESTRIAN SKILLS

Vikings were great horsemen. When not riding their hardy ponies into battle they liked nothing better than to practice their horseback-riding skills for pleasure. This silver pendant of a horseman from Sweden dates from the 10th century.

A FEASTING WE WILL GO

Feasts and festivals were a very common and popular form of entertainment, sometimes held in honor of the gods or for a great warrior. Originally they probably were held to celebrate the return of a raiding party, when the spoils were shared out. Feasts were usually held in the chieftain's hall but were not exclusive, all members of the community were welcome to attend. This illustration shows a huge vat of beer being prepared for a festival.

VÉRITABLE EXTRAIT DE VIANDE LIEBIG.

Histoire de la bière — 3.
Aegir comme brasseur et amphitryon.

Reproduction interdite.   Voir l'explication au verso.

BLOOD SPORTS

Many of the Vikings' outdoor pursuits were as much a test of a warrior's bravery as they were pastimes. Hunting was a popular activity, especially for dangerous animals such as bears. Warriors would often hunt on foot to prove their courage. Many Viking sports would be considered cruel by today's standards. They included blood sports such as bear baiting (where dogs were set upon a tethered bear) or horse fighting.

WINTER GAMES

During the long winter months many Vikings enjoyed outdoor sports, such as skiing and sledding. They also went skating on the frozen lakes and rivers using ice skates with blades made from carved bone or antlers.

BOARD GAMES

Board games were very popular with Vikings, especially with the men because many were based on war games. Particular favorites were chess and the similar game of "hnefatafl." In both games, players use pieces on a board to protect the king from attack. This beautifully carved chess set is made from carved bone, though sometimes ivory from walrus tusks was used. The pieces date from the late 12th century and are Norwegian in origin.

HEADDRESS

Women wore headbands or linen bonnets; men wore woolen caps. In the winter, both men and women wore fur-lined hats and gloves.

WOOLEN CAPE

Capes were made of thick wool, often brightly colored using vegetable dye. Sometimes they were embroidered or had fur trims.

FOOT LOOSE

Most shoes were made of goatskin with hardened leather or wooden soles. They were secured by a strap and buckle. In the winter, fur-lined leggings or overshoes were worn for extra warmth.

BODY WARMTH

Clothing was often loose-fitting to allow circulation of air between layers (which keeps one warmer) and held together with highly decorative pins, brooches, and buckles.

NATURAL FIBERS

Most clothes were made from wool or linen (fibers extracted from the crushed stems of the flax plant). Materials were thick and closely woven to give maximum warmth. Some quite intricate patterns were woven into the cloth. Common patterns were checks, similar to Scottish tartans, and geometric shapes. Sometimes pictures, such as animal heads, were included in the design.

UNDERGARMENTS

Women wore ankle-length linen under-dresses, often with a pinafore-style over-dress on top. Men wore knee-length tunics with woolen leggings beneath. Linen undergarments were also worn.

Fashion

Viking styles, generally, were unsophisticated; their prime concern was warmth and comfort. They were not a particularly fashion-conscious people, except as a means of showing one's position in society. Silver and gold jewelry, for instance, was often imported, which the rich wore as a kind of status symbol to display their wealth. They wore their clothes in layers to fend off the cold. Both rich and poor wore more or less the same style of clothes; the rich simply used better quality materials, sometimes imported silks and cottons. For most Vikings, clothes were purely functional with few concessions to decoration. On special occasions, wealthy Vikings might wear more elaborately embroidered tunics, perhaps with fur trims.

BELTING-UP

Leather belts were used to hold clothes at the waist or to support weapons. Buckles were usually moulded from metal, highly embossed or engraved for decoration. This belt end was made from carved bone.

BEADS and BROOCHES

The richly decorated brooch (above) would probably have held together the cape of a nobleman. The beads (left) were from a simple amber necklace.

ALL DRESSED UP

Vikings from all classes liked to wear ornate buckles and brooches, while the rich also liked to adorn themselves with fine jewelry, like this armband finished off with intricately carved dragon heads. Much Viking jewelry was imported or stolen, but this was made in Sweden in the 11th century.

Art and Architecture

The Viking homelands of Denmark, Norway, and Sweden were thickly forested, so it is perhaps not surprising that they chose to build with timber in preference to stone. Sadly, because of the vulnerability of wood to fire and damp, only remnants survive of their buildings and ornately carved woodwork, but it is enough to form a picture of their carpentry skills and artistry. Although no wooden churches survive from the main period of Viking activity (between the 8th and 11th centuries), several from the succeeding centuries of the medieval period do still stand, and they give us a good idea of what Viking buildings were like. The Vikings also produced finely crafted metalwork, but perhaps their greatest artistic legacy is in the carved stones they left behind using a combination of runes and pictograms. Many of these have religious significance, or tell stories from Nordic mythology, while others are memorial stones dedicated to the deeds of fallen warriors.

MEMORIAL STONES

Elaborately carved memorial stones are a striking feature of Viking art. They usually tell of heroic deeds performed by warriors. They were not placed on tombs, however, but in public places in celebration of the dead.

JEWELER'S ART

This magical amulet was worn on the chest, suspended from the neck on a chain, and was probably worn to ward off evil spirits. It shows how highly skilled the Vikings were at working metal into intricate shapes or molding pieces using molten metal. However, most jewelry was made for practical purposes, like brooches and dress pins used to hold items of clothing in place.

DOMESTIC ARCHITECTURE

Most ordinary people lived in small houses constructed of whole tree timbers (as shown here). As well as being easily available, timber was often warmer than stone in the cold Scandinavian climate.

VIKING HALLS

Every wealthy Viking lived in a large house, known as a hall. It had a central communal living room with an open fire, the smoke escaping through a louver in the roof. It would have been constructed solely of timber, sometimes with solid walls, sometimes with panels of plaster between uprights, and there would have been very few window openings to keep in the warmth. The roof was supported on timber columns and open to the rafters. Inside, the walls were often painted with scenes from mythology and the timber elaborately carved.

ELABORATE CARVING

Viking craftsmen never missed an opportunity to carve wood into elaborate designs, often depicting heroic exploits of warriors or scenes from mythology. This 12th century example comes from a stave church in Norway. These skills in wood carving were inherited by the Normans and adopted throughout Europe during the Middle Ages.

STAVE CHURCH

Following their conversion to Christianity around A.D. 960, Viking builders erected many wooden churches throughout Scandinavia. They built them in the same unique and distinctive style as their halls and houses, with elaborately carved wooden staves (planks or logs) set upright into the ground. Roofs were made of wooden tiles and arranged in tiers.

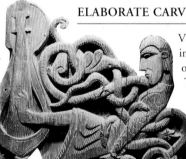

Health and Medicine

When the Roman Empire declined, a series of plagues and epidemics swept across the Roman world, allowing barbarian nations such as the Vikings to invade their strongholds in Europe. These barbarian nations saw the Roman approach to medicine, which was a more systematic and clinical approach based on study of the human anatomy, as the reason for Roman ruin — the gods had been offended. Therefore, medicine reverted to a more superstitious approach in these "dark ages," particularly in pagan lands such as Scandinavia at that time. To a large extent, Vikings saw illness and disease as weakness. Good health was intrinsically linked to religion. If the gods were properly honored, they would protect one from both injury and illness.

DIVINE INTERVENTION

Much of Viking medicine was still firmly rooted in superstition and religious divination. This wood carving from a stave church shows the mythical Sigurd divining the heart of a dragon, seeking answers from the gods by magical means. Such methods of diagnosis were commonly used in medicine.

COUNTRY DWELLERS

Although the bubonic plague affected most countries in Europe and the Middle East, the Vikings escaped the worst ravages of the disease. One of the reasons for this was probably their aversion to towns, preferring to live in small village communities in the country, which were less conducive to the spread of the disease.

HERBAL CURES

These margin illustrations from a manuscript show an apothecary (pharmacist) treating the sick and preparing remedies. Most Viking medicine took the form of herbal remedies using the plants that were readily available from the land. Common herbal cures in general use were red clover (to purify the blood), nettles (to improve the circulation), stinking arrach (to cure ulcers), eyebright (to cure eye infections), willow bark (to treat rheumatism brought on by the damp), and viper's bugloss (to treat snake bites).

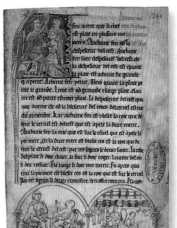

HEALTHY LIFESTYLE

By all accounts, the Vikings were a robust and strong race. Accounts of their raids in such writings as the *Anglo-Saxon Chronicle* describe them as being tall, broad and muscular. Most Vikings ate reasonably well and had plenty of physical exercise in the harsh, Scandinavian terrain, so they were probably healthier and hardier than many of their more southerly neighbors.

IN THE LAP OF THE GODS

Illness was often thought of as a punishment from the gods. Good health could be assured by pleasing them. Frey, and his sister Freyja (shown here), were gods of fertility, love, and birth. To ensure a healthy baby, pregnant women made offerings at their shrines.

BLOODLETTING

Bloodletting was a very ancient form of treating disease, still widely practiced in Viking times. Doctors believed that many illnesses were caused by an imbalance of the four humors (blood, yellow bile, black bile, and phlegm); the fluids they believed made up the human body. Letting out some of the blood was thought to cure this imbalance.

FIRSTBORN

This bronze figure of a woman is probably Freyja, goddess of fertility. It was customary for couples contemplating marriage to make an offering, or even a sacrifice, in her honor to ensure their own fertility. Although male Vikings treated their womenfolk well, it was still very much a patriarchal society and preference was always shown toward sons rather than daughters. It was important for the firstborn child to be a son; girls were often put to death.

BIGAMY

Until the advent of Christianity, bigamy was widely practiced in Viking society, although it was a privilege reserved only for the men (women could have only one husband). This picture shows a man exchanging wedding vows with a new wife while his existing wife looks on.

HEARTH and HOME

In Viking society the family, or kindred, was all-protecting. Any action or crime against one member of the family was, by custom, against the entire family. The custom also provided a crude form of social security because the kindred looked after a female member and her children should her husband die or be killed.

EMIGRATIONS

For many poorer Viking families, scarcity of land meant that the wives could not remain at home while their husbands were away on raiding expeditions. Instead, they accompanied their husbands, taking their possessions and children with them to set up home in the new colonies.

Love and Marriage

Despite the fact that Viking women were reasonably liberated, most marriages were not free choices but were arranged between both sets of parents. The marriage ceremony was divided into two stages.

The first was the wedding, or "pledging," when the two families would agree on terms for the bride-price. The bride's family would then hand over the agreed dowry to the groom's family. The second stage was the gift, or "giving-away," when the bride's father literally gave his daughter to the groom, followed by a feast paid for and held in the bride's father's house. Once married, Viking women acquired certain rights, including the right to hold their own land.

BRYNHILD

Brynhild was a beautiful Viking woman who, according to mythology, was a Valkyrie, a female warrior and messenger to Odin, god of war. Valkyries are sometimes represented as fearsome beings, at other times as beautiful maidens who offered their love and protection to warriors.

MAINTENANCE PAYMENTS

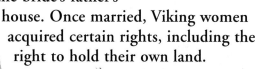

Until Vikings converted to Christianity, women reserved the right to divorce their husbands whenever they chose. More often than not, they did so simply because their spouse was not a good provider. If a husband divorced his wife, he was obliged to pay her compensation. If she left with the children, she was entitled to half the husband's wealth.

Women and Children

Women in Viking society enjoyed a high degree of freedom. Although men were still the ruling class and head of the family household, the women were independent-minded and strong-willed. When their husbands were away fighting on the many military campaigns, the running of the farms fell on their shoulders. During such times they undertook all of the duties normally performed by the men. On occasion, this might include taking up arms to fight. Although it is doubtful they took part in military attacks, they certainly helped the men defend Viking colonies when the need arose. The freedom enjoyed by Viking women even extended to attending the lawmaking assemblies (Things) where they were allowed to have their say. Children did not attend school but were expected to help with duties around the house and farm.

CONSOLIDATED GAINS

Women did not always stay at home while their husbands were away. Sometimes they accompanied them in the hope of acquiring land in one of the new colonies, especially if they were poor. They traveled with the men in the longships and sheltered somewhere safe until the fighting was over. This practice enabled the Vikings to establish strong footholds in other countries very quickly.

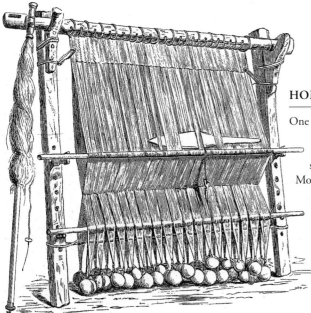

HOMESPUN

One of the principle duties of Viking women (and some men) was to make clothes for the family. They were skilled spinners and weavers of mostly wool and linen. Most households had a small, upright handloom (as shown here) which simply leaned against one wall of the house. Stones were used to weigh down the threads and keep them taut while the material was woven, employing some quite intricate designs.

A WARRIOR'S LIFE

From about the age of 12, boys began serious weapon training. Many went on raiding expeditions by the age of 16. There was no standing army, as such, but each man owed allegiance to his local chieftain and could be called upon to fight at any time. For boys from poor families, becoming a virtual full-time warrior was one means of escaping the poverty trap.

WELL GROOMED

Viking women were proud of their appearance, especially their hair. Long hair was fashionable, and they spent a great deal of time combing it. Combs were often made from intricately carved bone or antlers (shown left). The bone pins and spindle whorls, to the right, were used in spinning.

CHILDREN'S PLAYTHINGS

These wooden panpipes were probably a child's toy. Viking children played with a variety of wooden toys, such as dolls and soldiers, as well as board games. Children spent a great deal of time enjoying outdoor pursuits, including skiing and skating in the long winter months.

SURVIVAL OF THE FITTEST

Life in Viking society was hard. Weakness was not tolerated, not even in children. If a newborn baby was sickly and likely to be a liability for the family, the father reserved the right to expose it to the elements or cast it into the sea, where it soon died.

War and Weaponry

THE VALIANT WARRIOR

The valor with which Vikings fought was closely linked to their religious beliefs. They believed fallen warriors were transported to Asgard, home of the gods, where they fought alongside Odin, the chief of the gods. Each night they would be healed of their injuries and would feast in the hall of Valhalla (Viking heaven). The harder a warrior fought in this world, the more he would be favored by the gods in the afterlife.

Although the Vikings did settle in parts of Britain, France, Iceland, and Russia on a permanent basis, they were not seeking to conquer these lands. They were opportunist pirates who took advantage of the chaos following the collapse of the western Roman Empire in Europe. They were certainly warlike, but they were not barbarians, as is often depicted. They lived, for the most part, in an ordered and civilized society. Viking warriors, however, were feared throughout Europe for their ferocity. Viking warriors had no fear of death. If they died on the battlefield, it was considered an honorable death. To surrender or be taken prisoner would have brought shame and dishonor to their families.

The Viking speciality was to sail within sight of land and then, often by cover of darkness, slip unnoticed into river estuaries and creeks to make surprise attacks on villages further inland and less protected.

MENACING FIGUREHEADS

Vikings often carved menacing figureheads onto the bows of their ships and on the front of their sleighs (as left) to strike fear into the hearts of their enemies on approach or to protect themselves from evil. The figures might be mythical monsters, such as dragon heads, or representations of fierce warriors. The Vikings were a superstitious race and sometimes they carved the likeness of a deity, such as Thor, as protection in battle.

WARRIOR'S HELMET

Although popular fiction usually depicts Vikings wearing helmets adorned with animal horns, they were in fact the exception and not the rule, usually reserved for chieftains or for special occasions. The type of helmet worn by warriors was hornless and had either a noseplate or eyeguards for added protection. It was usually made from iron plates welded together, with a chain mail neck guard.

LONGSHIPS

Remains of Viking longships have been discovered in burial mounds and wrecks have been found to be deliberately sunk to block water channels. These discoveries have given us a good idea of what they looked like. They were well made, of clinker construction (overlapping boards to keep the water out), and varied in length from about 18–27 meters (60–90 ft) and from 2.7–5.2 meters (8–17 ft) wide. They were virtually flat-bottomed, but with a prominent keel (base) so they were very fast and could be landed with ease by beaching in narrow inlets, without the need for a quay.

BATTLE-AX

Although the battle-ax is the weapon most associated with Viking warriors, it was not in fact as common as the sword. Axes came in two basic forms: short-handled (mostly used as tools) and long-handled (used as weapons). These were held with two hands and swung around the head in battle. The ax heads were made of iron and were often highly decorated with wooden handles.

FAVORITE WEAPONS

Swords were the favorite weapon of most Viking warriors and were treated as prize possessions. It was common for a warrior to be buried with his sword to take with him into the afterlife to continue the battle. In Scandinavian mythology, swords were endowed with magical powers and were given highly evocative names, such as "killer." Swords were usually single-handed but double-edged, and were made of iron. Other popular weapons were bow and arrows and spears for both throwing (which were lighter and more slender) and thrusting. The weapons shown here are a typical sword and a thrusting spear; both date from the 8th century. Most warriors also carried a circular shield, made of wood with a central iron boss, sometimes fitted with a spike for thrusting at the enemy.

Crime and Punishment

The Vikings were not as lawless as one might suppose and actually operated a very democratic form of government that involved ordinary men in the lawmaking process. Unusual for the time, even the wives of chieftains and freemen were allowed to give their opinions. Most crimes were punishable by compensation, but if the victim or their family refused payment of money, they reserved the right to exact revenge upon the perpetrator of a crime or his family. A complex system of compensation existed from theft right through to murder.

Trial by combat or by ordeal (such as walking on red hot cinders) were also common, for Vikings believed the innocent would be protected by the gods. Each year at the annual assembly the Law Speaker recited aloud all the laws to ensure everyone knew them.

DEATH BY STRANGULATION

This unfortunate man died by ritual strangulation. He was discovered preserved in a peat bog in Denmark with the rope still around his neck. It may have been a revenge killing (as punishment by the victim's family) for committing murder, or it may have been a religious sacrifice; both animal and human sacrifices featured in Viking religion.

EXTORTION

In the late 10th century, the Vikings, having consolidated their position at home, renewed their attacks on England with a vengeance. The combined forces of Olaf, king of Norway, and Sweyn, king of Denmark, wrought havoc once more on English towns. They agreed to leave only on payment of a bribe, called Danegeld (Dane-gold), exacted from the taxpayers.

THE ALTHING

Once a year a national assembly met to make decisions of government. This was called an Althing. The main picture shows such a meeting place in Iceland, called the Thingvellir ("Parliament Plains"), which was the site of the first meeting in A.D. 930.

THE THING

Vikings operated a fairly free and democratic society. Local chieftains ruled over small regions, but they were controlled by an assembly, called a Thing. Here every freeman had the right to have his say on all issues ranging from local disputes, compensation claims, and matters of government and law. One such assembly was at Tynwald Hill on the Isle of Man (a Viking colony) where the modern government of this island still sits.

TRAVELING FAR AND WIDE

The Vikings traveled great distances in their search for land and treasure. Wherever possible, they did so by water. Their ships were comparatively light and easily transportable and could be carried overland between rivers. They exploited much of western Russia this way, reaching as far south as the Mediterranean and even reaching the Middle East. This bronze figure of a Buddha was brought back to Sweden from a trading expedition to northern India.

In the west, they reached as far as North America.

BRIDGING THE GAP

The Vikings were great bridge builders. Their mountainous terrain was crisscrossed with many watercourses, which made transport difficult. It was the responsibility of the local population to keep its bridges in good repair. Bridges were normally constructed of wood, though some were built of stone.

YOUR CARRIAGE AWAITS

This Viking wagon was discovered in the Oseberg ship grave and dates from the 9th century. It is heavily constructed of wood and is typical of wagons used at that time. The upper carriage was, like so much else in the Viking world, heavily carved with mythical symbols. The wheels are interesting in that, instead of being solid circles of wood (more usual for the time), they have a sturdy rim and spokes, giving maximum strength but less weight.

Transport and Science

The Vikings were not always the uncultivated, bloodthirsty warriors that history has portrayed them. Mostly they were farmers and settlers with a bold spirit of adventure, seeking out new lands, and were highly skilled metal- and woodworkers. They were something of a "magpie" society in that, although they brought few new innovations to the countries they invaded and settled, they quickly adapted to the ways of their host nations and absorbed many of the ideas they encountered into their own way of life. However, they did invent, or certainly develop, the use of skis and ice skates to travel around the frozen landscape in the winter. The Vikings maintained a reasonably good network of roads (mostly in the form of tracks) and bridges, essential in the often inhospitable terrain of their northerly homelands. Bridges also assumed a religious significance and were often associated with the journey to the afterlife. Viking mythology contains many references to legendary heroes who protected bridges from attack.

TRADING PLACES

The Vikings were great traders, even more so than they were great pirates. They opened up many trade routes, exchanging their timber, iron, furs, and animal skins for more exotic goods, such as silver and gold, silk and jewels. Always astute businessmen, wherever they went Viking traders took finely crafted scales with them, usually made of bronze and transported in specially made carrying cases.

CARGO BOATS

The Vikings were expert navigators and shipbuilders. The seas were largely uncharted and they found their way navigating by the sun and stars. They used two main types of boat: longships for war and knarrs for fishing and trading. Both were open, clinker-built (overlapping planks), and propelled by a combination of oars and a central square sail. They had strong keels (the base, or backbone, of a ship) that cut through the water easily, making them incredibly seaworthy. They were steered by a rudder or steering board on the right-hand side of the ship, from where the term "starboard" (meaning to the right of a ship) is believed to have derived.

SLEIGH RIDE

One of the principle means of getting around the frozen landscape in winter was by sled, pulled by teams of dogs. They were quite large, about the same size as a wagon, but with two wooden blades instead of wheels to enable speedy transport through the snow and ice. They were often decorated with ornate wood carvings, like this one.

Religion

There were many different gods in Viking religion. Many began as simple nature spirits but gradually evolved into a complex mythology, telling stories of heroic, warrior-like gods that reflected their own lifestyle. The three most important gods were Odin, Thor, and Frey. Odin was chief of the gods and symbolized, among other things, war, courage, and wisdom. Thor was the god of thunder, while Frey was the god of fertility. Vikings thought of their gods in much the same way as they viewed themselves, fighting against the powers of evil and darkness. Strangely, however, they also believed that they and their gods were fighting a lost cause, doomed to failure. It was this belief that was largely responsible for the heroism of Viking warriors, for by dying a hero's death on earth they could join the gods in Valhalla, the Viking heaven, and continue the struggle there.

OLD AND NEW

For many years the recently converted Vikings did not fully accept Christianity and continued to worship their old gods alongside the new faith. This amulet in the shape of Thor's hammer also incorporates Christian symbolism.

MISCHIEVOUS LOKI

Loki is a strange creature in Norse mythology, part god and part devil. He seems to have created mischief wherever he went and was instigator of discord among the gods. He is often associated with fire and blacksmiths' forges. He is seen here on a forge stone with his lips sewn together, having tried to trick a dwarf blacksmith.

GOD OF FERTILITY

Frey, one of the most important Viking gods, was god of fertility. His sister Freyja was the goddess of fertility and love. They were at the center of a powerful cult and newly married couples looked to them to bless their union. Vikings worshipped the individual gods in their own right but also collectively as a kind of family of gods.

CHRISTIANITY ARRIVES

The Vikings became influenced by Christianity on their raiding expeditions to lands in western Europe. King Harald Bluetooth converted Denmark to Christianity around A.D. 960, with Norway and Sweden following a century later. At first Christianity was seen simply as a way of strengthening ties with other Christian countries; tradesmen wearing crucifixes were usually allowed free passage. Canute, who became king of Denmark, Norway, and England in 1016 was a Christian who rebuilt many of the churches destroyed by his pagan ancestors.

THOR, GOD OF THUNDER

Thor is one of the great heroes of Viking mythology. He was the god of thunder and carried a mighty silver hammer possessed of magical powers. When he used it to strike an enemy, thunder was heard in the heavens. Thor rode through the sky in a magnificent chariot, championing the poor. He symbolized everything a good Viking warrior should strive to be.

EARTH MOTHER

In the Bronze Age, the Vikings worshipped the sun, the Earth Mother (goddess of fertility and rebirth), and nature spirits. They worshipped in the open, such as at springs or in forest clearings. This picture shows the winter solstice festival, which celebrates the shortest day and the return of the sun. Human sacrifices were not uncommon; sometimes the widows of fallen warriors would offer themselves as sacrifices so they could join their husbands in Valhalla.

Legacy of the Past

DAYS OF THE WEEK

Several days of the week are named after Viking gods. Tuesday is named after Tyr, the Viking god of war (shown above with a tethered animal). Wednesday is named after Woden (or Odin), while his wife, Frigga, gave her name to Friday. Thursday is named after the thunder god, Thor.

The Vikings have left little evidence of their existence, but perhaps the finest monument of the Viking age is Ales Stenar in Skane, Sweden (see main picture). To some extent, the strongest influence of the Vikings was not felt directly but from the descendants of one of their colonies, the Normans, who had settled in an area of northern France known as Normandy. Under them, Europe suffered a further wave of invasions. The influence of the Normans was felt for several centuries afterward and greatly influenced the political and cultural direction taken by most countries in medieval Europe. Perhaps the greatest legacy left behind by the Vikings, however, is their rich tapestry of mythology and epic poems, every bit as complex and colorful as that of the Greeks and Romans. Nordic stories and poems are among the finest works of literature to survive from the Dark Ages.

THE NORMANS

In 911 a Norwegian prince called Rolf (or Rollo) invaded northern France with a mixed (mainly Danish) Viking army. The French king, Charles the Simple, offered them an area of France in return for peace. This area became known as Normandy (land of the North, or Norsemen). The Treaty of Claire-sur-Epte gave Rolf a dukedom, subject to the French king. Rolf and his followers soon settled and adopted many French ways, eventually forming a powerful nation in their own right. This scene, from the Bayeux Tapestry, shows the Norman's conquest of England in the 11th century. Their boats show the direct influence of the Viking longboats.

AMERICAN SETTLEMENTS

Although North America had long been settled by aboriginal Indian tribes, the Vikings were probably the first Europeans to land and settle there. Leif Eriksson (the Lucky) was the first recorded Viking to land in America (though there may have been others). He discovered the Newfoundland coast in what is now part of Canada, in 1001. He is said to have made his discovery by accident when his ships were blown off course en route for Greenland, another Viking colony. He called this new land Vinland, and it is assumed that this was because he believed the wild berries that grew there were grape vines.

Later Viking adventurers may also have discovered Labrador and Baffin Island. The Vikings found the natives hostile, however, and never formed a permanent settlement there.

DID YOU KNOW?

That the term "going berserk" is derived from the Vikings? One of the Viking gods of war was Tyr. He is often depicted wearing a bearskin cloak with the bear's head draped over his helmet. The Viking word for "bearskin" was "berserk" and a special class of warrior, all dressed in bearskins, came to be known as "berserkirs." They used to work themselves up into a rage before going into battle, from where the modern term "going berserk," is derived. The frenzy may have been drug-induced.

That the Vikings were head hunters? Many pagan religions held the skull to be sacred and believed that it housed a person's soul. Viking warriors are known to have hacked off the heads of their fallen enemies, partly as trophies of war and partly to capture the valor of their dead spirits by using their skulls as drinking vessels.

That Father Christmas may have his origins in Norse mythology? Like most other religions, when Christianity was adopted as the main faith of the Western world, it acquired many of the customs and festivals of its preceding pagan religions. One of these was the Viking custom of giving presents at the time of the winter solstice. Odin, like the Saxon god Woden, used to career across the night sky in a chariot bearing gifts. When this festival was Christianized, the feast day of Saint Nicholas (the patron saint of children) was borrowed, from where the name "Santa Claus" is derived.

That the kingdoms of England and Scotland did not exist at the time of the first Viking raids? The Viking raids on Britain in the 8th and 9th centuries were instrumental in forming the two countries we know today as England and Scotland. Until then, both countries were made up of several independent kingdoms, who often fought among themselves for superiority. As the threat of a full-scale Viking invasion became more imminent, these individual warring nations united to fend off the attack. In 843 Kenneth MacAlpin became the first king of Scotland when he united the Picts and the Scots. In 827 Ecgberht first united England under a single crown, consolidated by Alfred the Great in 871.

That Norse mythology may have inspired Tolkien to write *The Hobbit*? Although the children's fantasy novel *The Hobbit*, and its epic sequel *The Lord of the Rings*, are works of pure fiction, their author, J.R.R. Tolkien, drew upon his intimate knowledge of Norse mythology when he created the Hobbits and the kingdom of Middle Earth. Dwarfs and runes figure prominently in the stories, as do several other Scandinavian elements, including place names and magic, all of which feature prominently in Viking myths.

ACKNOWLEDGMENTS
We would like to thank: Graham Rich and Elizabeth Wiggans for their assistance and David Hobbs for his map of the world.
Picture research by Image Select.
First edition for the United States, Canada, and the Philippines published by Barron's Educational Series, Inc., 1998
First published in Great Britain in 1998 by *ticktock* Publishing Ltd., The office, The Square, Hadlow, Kent, TN11 0DD, United Kingdom
Copyright © 1998 by *ticktock* Publishing, Ltd.

All inquiries should be addressed to:
Barron's Educational Series, Inc.
250 Wireless Boulevard Hauppauge, New York 11788 http://www.barronseduc.com
Library of Congress Catalog Card No. 98-72966   International Standard Book No. 0-7641-0631-7
Printed in Hong Kong

987654321

Picture Credits:
t=top, b=bottom, c=center, l=left, r=right, IFC=inside front cover, OBC=outside back cover, OFC=outside front cover

AKG (London): 2/3c, 4/5b & 32ct, 5tr & IFC, 10/11c, 14/15t, 16/17c, 18bl, 18c, 18/19c, 19tr, 20tl, 21tr, 22tl, 26cr, 28/29b. Ann Ronan Picture Library; 8b. Ann Ronan/Image Select; 6tl, 7b, 8tl, 8/9c, 11cr, 11tr, 17cb, 22/23cb. Ancient Art and Architecture Collection/R. Sheridan; 5cb, 23cb, 27cr. Bridgeman Art Library; 31cr. Bridgeman/Giraudon; 17tr, 21br, 21/22r. CFCL/Image Select; 6/7c, 9br, 15br. e.t.archive/Bibliotheque Nationale; 16bl. Giraudon; 4/5c, 14/15b, 31tr. Image Select; 8/9b, 20bl. Knudsens Fotosenter/Giraudon; 22bl, 27cb. PIX; 9tr, 14tl, 23tr, 26c, 30/31(background pic). Spectrum Colour Library; 25c. Werner Forman Archive; 2bl, 3cr, 3br, 4tl, 6br, 7tr, 10bl, 10tr, 13br, 13cb, 14bl, 15cl, 16tl, 17cr, 19br, 23bl, 24tl, 24/25c, 24/25(background pic), 26tl, 27cr, 28bl, 28tl, 28/29c, 29r, 30tl.York Archaeological Trust; 2tl, 6bl, 12bl, 12tl, 13tr, 12/13b, 21cr.

Every effort has been made to trace the copyright holders and we apologize in advance for any unintentional omissions.
We would be pleased to insert the appropriate acknowledgment in any subsequent edition of this publication.

BARRON'S